constructive
feedback

ROLAND AND
FRANCES BEE

Roland and Frances Bee are directors of Time *for* People Ltd, a personnel and training consultancy specialising in customer care, time/self-management, and in training needs analysis and evaluation. Together they combine a wide range of professional and management experience in retail, financial services and in local authorities. They have worked with a broad range of clients in both the public and private sectors – particularly in retail, transportation, electronics and the universities. In addition to *Constructive Feedback*, Roland and Frances Bee are co-authors of *Training Needs Analysis and Evaluation* (1994), *Customer Care* (1995), *Project Management: The people challenge* (1997), *Facilitation Skills* (1998), and *Managing Information and Statistics* (1999), all published by the Chartered Institute of Personnel and Development.

Management Shapers is a comprehensive series covering all the crucial management skill areas. Each book includes the key issues, helpful starting points and practical advice in a concise and lively style. Together, they form an accessible library reflecting current best practice – ideal for study or quick reference.

The Chartered Institute of Personnel and Development is the leading publisher of books and reports for personnel and training professionals, students, and all those concerned with the effective management and development of people at work. For full details of all our titles, please contact the Publishing Department:

tel. 020-8263 3387
fax 020-8263 3850
e-mail publish@cipd.co.uk

The catalogue of all CIPD titles can be viewed on the CIPD website:
www.cipd.co.uk/publications

constructive
feedback

ROLAND AND
FRANCES BEE

CHARTERED INSTITUTE OF PERSONNEL AND DEVELOPMENT

© Roland and Frances Bee 1996

First published in the *Training Extras* series in 1996
First published in the *Management Shapers* series in 1998
Reprinted 2000

Typesetting by Paperweight
Printed in Great Britain by
The Guernsey Press, Channel Islands

British Library Cataloguing in Publication Data
A catalogue record for this book is available from the
British Library

ISBN
0-85292-752-5

Chartered Institute of Personnel and Development, CIPD House,
Camp Road, London SW19 4UX
Tel.: 020 8971 9000   Fax: 020 8263 3333
E-mail: cipd@cipd.co.uk   Website: www.cipd.co.uk
Incorporated by Royal Charter. Registered charity no. 1079797

contents

Other titles in the series:

introduction

Feedback is a fundamental part of the process of leading people towards behaviour and performance that are appropriate to any given situation. We receive feedback all the time:

- informally in our everyday interactions, from people reacting to what we have said or done

- more formally from our boss commenting on our work, from our staff responding to the way we manage them, from our colleagues, customers, and suppliers

- on training courses, helping us to learn new skills

- from our environment, when as children we might have been attracted to the warm, rosy glow of a fire in the room but learned from the feedback of burning our fingers that heat is safe only at a distance

- from ourselves, eg from

  O knowing how much stress we can absorb

  □ reflecting on how we feel about the things we do and that others do.

Feedback on how we are doing is essential for us to learn and grow. It gives the opportunity to vary our approach and work harder if necessary – to produce a better result. Successful people in all walks of life are aware of the feedback they receive all the time from bosses, subordinates, colleagues, customers, suppliers and their environment, and have learned to use it. They actively seek it. Equally, they see the need to provide feedback, but in a way that enhances performance and relationships. The skills of being able to give constructive feedback, to receive and use feedback, are vital in the workplace. They are just as useful in social settings and in the home!

This book is aimed at helping you identify:

- when to give feedback
- how to give constructive feedback
- how to receive and use feedback for yourself.

Chapter 1 explains what we mean by constructive feedback, distinguishing this from destructive criticism, and Chapter 2 examines how constructive feedback can be used in many workplace scenarios. Chapter 3 is the heart of this book – explaining how to give constructive feedback and providing 10 'tools' of guidance. Chapter 4 looks at some particularly challenging feedback situations, suggesting strategies that will help. Chapter 5 covers an often overlooked skill – how to solicit constructive feedback yourself and benefit fully from it. Finally, Chapter 6 sets out how to continuously improve your constructive feedback skills.

1 what is constructive feedback?

What is feedback?

Feedback is an integral part of two-way communication. It is the link between the things you do and say, and understanding the impact these have on others. In terms of influencing people at work it is, perhaps, the most important interpersonal skill that you can develop. In our view it is the characteristic that differentiates between:

- managers who successfully motivate and develop their staff and those who struggle in their people-management role

- coaches and advisers who really succeed in improving performance and those who just skim the surface

- ▲ trainers who effectively impart skills that are transferred into the workplace and those who just run training courses

- mentors who release potential and those who stifle it

- people who make effective team members and those who get in the way of team performance.

Feedback has been defined as:

- ● 'information about performance or behaviour that leads to an action to affirm or develop that performance or behaviour'[1]

- ■ 'letting trainees know what they have done [that] has reached the standard, so that they can reproduce that behaviour, and what they have done [that] has not reached the standard, so that plans can be agreed with them on how to prevent a recurrence of that behaviour and how to progress to the required standard'.[2]

What is key about these definitions is that they assume the person receiving the feedback can actually do something right or, if not, there is a positive way forward to getting it right. In other words, the assumption is that feedback is *constructive*: it is about building on what is good and planning further development.

The difference between (constructive) feedback and (destructive) criticism

Feedback can either be *positive* – reinforcing 'good' performance and behaviours – or *negative* – correcting and improving 'poor' performance and behaviours. Both types of feedback can, and must, be constructive. The two major problems are:

- ● a lack of positive feedback – there is no recognition or affirmation of good performance

■ negative feedback provided in such a way that it becomes *destructive criticism*.

Destructive criticism tends to occur when feedback is given only when things go wrong (does this sound familiar?) and when there are no agreed standards against which to measure behaviour or performance, or any plan for development. It tends to come in the form of generalised, subjective comments, often focusing on personal traits or perceived attitudes, rather than in the form of objective comments focusing on specific examples of behaviours. For example, telling someone 'I don't like your attitude' is destructive criticism. Instead you need to comment on the behaviours that are causing the problem, providing specific examples. Criticism can be very destructive to personal relationships and to any prospective development strategy. Where there are agreed standards of behaviour and performance, and two-way communication about what has gone right as well as what has gone wrong, there is feedback that we define as *constructive feedback*.

The purpose of feedback

So, in summary, constructive feedback:

● provides information about behaviour and performance against objective standards in such a way that recipients maintain a positive attitude towards themselves and their work

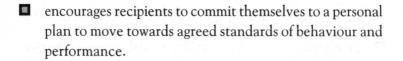
■ encourages recipients to commit themselves to a personal plan to move towards agreed standards of behaviour and performance.

Feedback is intrinsically linked to the learning process. Essentially, when you give feedback you are helping someone to learn – learn, that is, new knowledge and skills or improved behaviours and performance.

When and where to give feedback

We believe that constructive feedback is needed as a regular and constant part of everyday communication among managers and their staff, members of teams, parents and children, spouses, and friends. Unfortunately, what happens in many workplaces is that a mass of negative feedback is 'saved up' for the annual appraisal. Then, when it is given, it suffers from the dual sins of being too much and too late. The recipient is buried under the weight of these criticisms, which often relate to issues and events that happened long ago, and which the recipient cannot recall clearly and over which he or she no longer has any influence.

In general terms, so far as the timing of feedback is concerned, the golden rules are to:

● give feedback close to the event(s) to which it refers: the event(s) will be fresher in the minds of both the recipient and the giver, and therefore the feedback is likely to be more specific, better understood, and easier

to incorporate into future work

■ take into account your ability to deliver constructive feedback at that time, ie do you have the time, do you feel relaxed and confident?

▲ take into account the recipient's ability to handle the feedback: is he or she full up with feedback, under too much pressure?

The 'where' of giving feedback is perhaps obvious. In the workplace, it is generally best to seek a quiet room where you will not be overheard or interrupted. Of course, there is no harm in giving general praise in front of others (indeed there are considerable benefits). However, the greatest benefits are gained when the praise is linked to specific performance and it is clear why the praise has been given, ie what specifically was good about the performance or behaviour.

In the training situation, there are often two options:

● one-to-one between trainer and trainee in a quiet room – appropriate if the feedback is of a particularly sensitive nature or where the trainee may have difficulty handling it in an open forum

■ in the training group, with other participants in the learning exercise, who can often add a wider perception of the event than can be given by one person, and where mutual learning can take place from listening to feedback to and from other trainees.

Barriers to giving and receiving feedback

Several factors get in the way of constructive feedback whether you are giving it or are on the receiving end. Some people feel inadequate or awkward when called upon to comment on the performance of others at work. There are some basic barriers to contend with:

- Feedback can come as a surprise or shock when there are no clear objectives for the job, or when the employee and supervisor do not share the same perception of what the job entails.

- There may be barriers to communication, eg a poor personal relationship between the employee and supervisor.

- The feedback may be delivered in a way that the recipient sees as criticism, ie as concentrating on critical or unsubstantiated judgements which offend against the recipient's sense of fairness.

- There may be a problem of credibility: it is important that the recipient believes the feedback-giver is competent to comment on those points.

- Previous history of receiving negative feedback may make the recipient feel obliged to 'defend his or her corner'.

- It is often more comfortable to hide behind excuses to avoid giving feedback, such as:

  O people know whether they are doing a good job or not, and do not need to be told

☐ they will get upset if they are told they are not doing a good job, and do it even worse; better to let sleeping dogs lie

△ if you tell people they are doing well they will become complacent or ask for a pay rise

○ it creates more hassle and extra work than it is worth, and you are too busy already.

◼ People are 'afraid' to give feedback because they are not confident about handling the response.

▲ People are concerned that feedback will damage relationships.

Fortunately, all these barriers (and many others) can be overcome, as we shall demonstrate. Giving and receiving feedback is a skill which, like any other, can be developed. In the next chapter we hope to help you towards your goal of achieving excellence in this vital communication skill.

Throughout this book there are exercises for you to complete. We suggest you set up a logbook to record the results of these exercises and monitor the development of your feedback skills.

Exercise 1

Reflect on and record in your logbook:

○ how you feel about giving and receiving feedback: jot down the factors that make giving and receiving feedback difficult for you

▫ whether you give feedback when it is needed and, if not, why not

△ whether you welcome feedback on yourself and, if not, why not.

References

1 THATCHER, JOHN. 'Motivating people via feedback', *Training and Development (UK)*, Vol 12 No 7, July 1994. pp 8–10, 12.

2 RUSSELL, TIM. *Effective Feedback Skills*. London, Kogan Page, 1994.

2 using constructive feedback

We look next at some areas where constructive feedback is important in your various roles – as a manager in maintaining and improving performance, as coach and counsellor, trainer, mentor and team player. Last, but by no means least, we look at the role that constructive feedback can play in improving morale, motivation, and commitment. We examine some scenarios that illustrate the importance of constructive feedback, and some common pitfalls. From the scenarios we begin to identify the key principles of giving feedback, which will be developed in Chapter 3.

Maintaining and improving performance

Maintaining and improving performance is rather like piloting an aeroplane between two places. The sooner we obtain information on how much we are deviating from our desired route, the smaller the navigational correction needed to take us to our destination. So it is with maintaining and improving performance: the sooner we know how well we are doing, the smaller the change required in our method of working to achieve our objective. Given early, constructive feedback will be more effective and less 'painful' than if given later. Early feedback can be described as 'a light hand on the tiller'. Early, minor corrections to performance can make the need for major changes in performance unlikely.

Scenario 1

Terry is sweeping a warehouse prior to inspection by the manager at the end of the day. Let us assume that the warehouse will take about four hours to sweep out. After about three and a half hours his supervisor says, 'Haven't you finished yet? We'll never be ready for the inspection now. Look at these aisles, they're filthy!'

Would you describe these comments as constructive feedback? It is easy to understand the supervisor's frustration with someone who is not performing and therefore letting the team down, but is this feedback likely to improve Terry's performance? There are two problems:

- Feedback is being given so late that it is almost impossible for the fault to be remedied.

- The feedback is destructive, not constructive: it says what is wrong, but in a very generalised way; it provides no help on what the standards of cleanliness are or any suggestions for improvement.

Consider this alternative approach:

The supervisor says to Terry after about half an hour, 'Terry, it's good to see you making progress. However, to finish in good time you need to complete each row in about 20 minutes. Also, the standard required is that all litter must be removed and although you are shifting a lot of rubbish, you are missing some in the corners. You might find it helpful to use a smaller brush in these areas. Remember that the job must be completed by 4.00pm for inspection by the warehouse manager. I will pop back in half an hour to see how you are getting on.'

Basically, all constructive feedback lets recipients know:

- what the standards are

- how they are doing

- what they need to change in order to meet the standards

- how long they have to improve

- what support they can expect from you.

Most managers appreciate the need to take action where performance is not up to standard, but what about the situation where someone is doing well? Do you breathe a sigh of relief and move on to a more pressing matter? It is equally important to provide feedback to someone doing a good job, because:

- people need to know that they are performing to standard: a surprisingly large number of people worry if nothing is said

- it is motivating to be praised or caught 'doing something right'[1]

- it is important that people understand what specifically is good about their work, as this could be an area for further challenge

- it is rare for someone's work to be good in every respect, so commenting on what has gone well affords the opportunity to give that 'light hand on the tiller' mentioned earlier to the areas where performance could be improved.

Scenario 2

Jane's manager is very pleased with her work and says, 'Your report on the market research survey on customers' response to the new store was excellent. It was well structured, clearly written, and produced on time. In your next report you might consider including more diagrams rather than tables to help communicate the main points. What do you think?'

Here we have some specific praise – what was particularly good about the report – and some suggestions for further improvement. In addition, and very importantly, the manager is not imposing his or her views but seeking to open up a dialogue on the best way forward. Constructive feedback should always be two-way, allowing the recipient to probe the comments and be involved in the decision-making for further action.

The process of managing performance and behaviour is ongoing, with feedback occurring as and when required. The feedback skills are the same whether formal or informal processes are used (see later in this chapter).

Coaching and counselling

This could be considered the next stage after the 'light hand on the tiller', where more directed help is required and where there are gaps in knowledge, skills or behaviours that need addressing, eg as part of the NVQ/SVQ process of developing people in the workplace. It is not the purpose of this book to describe coaching or counselling skills in any detail but to emphasise the key role played by constructive feedback.

Scenario 3

Susan operates a check-out in a department store. She was trained to use the till but is making mistakes processing cheques. Joan, her supervisor, decides that some coaching would be appropriate. She demonstrates what needs to be done to deal with the cheques and then asks Susan to have a go. Susan makes some mistakes and Joan says, 'No, no, no! You've done it wrong again! You must watch closely and concentrate on what you are doing. Let me show you again.'

What do you think? Yes, a pretty dire piece of feedback. The problems are clear:

- No specific information is given on what mistakes have been made.

- There is no clear indication about what should be done differently.

- No standards are given for processing cheques.

- It is certainly not a case of two-way communication!

Counselling is a different process from coaching: feedback is less directed, with the emphasis on helping the individual work his or her way through the problem. The aim, by the skilful use of questions, is to explore issues and get the individual to come up with his or her solution(s). Consider Scenario 4.

Scenario 4

Sharon has just joined the section, and although she works to a good standard she is consistently abrupt and irritable with her colleagues. Joan, her supervisor, has decided that she must speak to Sharon. She asks Sharon to join her in the interview room, which is quiet and where there will be no interruptions. Joan starts by saying, 'I am pleased with the quality of your work; however, on occasions you speak very curtly to your colleagues. For example, when David asked you for the budget file yesterday you told him that you were too busy to look for it and then went back to your work.' Depending on Sharon's reaction, Joan could continue with such questions as, 'How do you think David felt about it?' 'How else could you have dealt with David's request?' 'How do you feel about working in the section?' 'What help do you need from me to settle into the section?'

Joan gave very specific feedback on the behaviour that was causing the problem – not by using words like 'irritable', but by describing the behaviour she had observed. The example was very recent – it had happened the day before. Joan put it into the context of Sharon's overall performance: Sharon was generally doing well – however, there was one area of difficulty. The emphasis was then on drawing the issues and answers out from Sharon, rather than telling her specifically what to do. In this way Sharon is encouraged to think through the problem for herself and come up with solutions. This has the double advantage that Sharon is in fact best placed to generate the solutions and is likely to feel a much greater sense of ownership of 'her' solution. She is more likely to implement this solution than one that has been 'imposed' upon her.

Learning new competencies

The use of constructive feedback in maintaining and improving performance, and in counselling and coaching has been described above. When learning new competencies we are perhaps at our most open to receiving feedback. We are familiar with receiving feedback when we are learning something new in a formal training or education setting – whether informally during and after practical exercises or formally, by examination. Feedback in the training situation is a vital part of the learning process, providing essential information to trainees on how they are progressing and what else they need to do to achieve the learning objective.

The potential for giving feedback is often great – and not just from trainers but also from other trainees. Indeed, trainees can provide very powerful feedback, particularly on behaviours that have directly affected them. In interview training, for example, the feedback from a trainee who has role-played the interviewee, or from team members in a team-building exercise, is highly relevant. However, it is also feedback that can go badly wrong and it is essential to manage it sensitively.

Scenario 5

Fiona has role-played someone being interviewed for selection by another trainee, Frank. It was a poor interview with insufficient probing, so a lot of important information was missed. Afterwards Fiona comments, 'That was fine, Frank: I felt very relaxed and comfortable.'

The trainer has a double issue here: Frank needs some constructive feedback to improve his interviewing skills and Fiona needs some help to improve her feedback skills. What do you think about the following approach?

The trainer asks Frank to summarise the information that he has obtained from the interview and then asks Fiona if there is any additional information contained in her brief that Frank has not brought out. This provides clear, observable evidence that information has been missed. The trainer then asks both of them to think about the sorts of questions that could have generated the missing information. Next, the trainer thanks Fiona for her feedback but suggests she expand on it by asking her to comment on what Frank did that made her feel relaxed and comfortable. Finally, the trainer makes clear how useful the additional information is, because Frank now knows what specific behaviours led to the positive outcome of his interviewee feeling comfortable and relaxed.

In this way, the trainer draws out of both Frank and Fiona what needs improvement – in Frank's case, his interviewing skills and in Fiona's her feedback skills.

Developing and releasing potential

Perhaps the most difficult, but also one of the most important, roles for a manager is to help staff develop and realise their potential. Sometimes this role is played outside the line structure by a 'mentor'. Skilled and well-presented feedback is a crucial part of this process. Realising your potential may simply be a matter of expanding your present job, eg discovering that you are really good at making presentations when your manager provides the opportunity for you to use that skill. Alternatively, it may rest on a longer-term and wider-reaching basis affecting your whole career. A skilled mentor or coach can help you see beyond your current performance and clarify opportunities and career paths. Constructive feedback at key stages in individuals' careers can ensure that their *potential* is transformed into *actual performance*.

Scenario 6

Carol is keen to progress within her organisation and decides to apply for every vacancy at the next level. She is unsuccessful and is beginning to believe that sexism might be a factor in her lack of progression; she is becoming very bitter about that. Let's look at a scene where Carol has just returned from her latest failure to secure promotion and discusses this with two potential mentors.

Mentor A: 'I know it's tough: promotion is hard to get these days. Don't get despondent, keep on trying: I know you are well respected. It took me several years to get my promotion. You must be patient.'

Mentor B: 'Let's look at what you want to achieve. What's important to you: the money, the status, or developing the new skills? Look at your strengths and those areas where you feel improvement is needed. This will help target the jobs you might be most suited to and identify areas for further training and development. Alternatively, we might look at strategies for extending your experience, such as project work or a secondment. It might also be helpful to see if you can get some feedback on how you performed at interview, in case your interview skills need some attention.'

Which mentor is the more likely to unlock Carol's full potential?

Developing team performance

Teamworking is fundamental to the success of most organisations. Increasingly, you will work as a member of several teams, and change teams far more frequently than in the past. This is partly because the structure of the workplace is changing, with less use of formal and rigid structures, but more use of flexible, project-based teams. The ability of team members to give one another constructive feedback is a key ingredient in this process.

Scenario 7

A project team has just been set up to look at ways of improving customer service. It consists of representatives from all departments. At the project meetings, Steven from the marketing department is dominating the discussion with his ideas, with the result that other members of the team are becoming frustrated at not being allowed the opportunity of contributing their own ideas. Susan from the production department decides to tackle Steven during the meeting:

'Hang on a minute, Steven, you're always pushing your ideas and none of us are getting a look-in! Why don't you just keep quiet for a few minutes and listen to the rest of us – we have ideas, too, you know.'

This might work in the short term: Steven might shut up. But it probably will not do much to help team performance. Steven may well decide to opt out all together or become very destructive of others' ideas. A more productive approach might be for Susan to speak to Steven informally outside the meeting.

'Steven, I would value a few minutes with you to discuss how the project meetings are going.' She might then seek his views or get straight to the point: 'You have some excellent ideas, which you present very effectively. However, I am finding it difficult to contribute my own ideas. For example, at this morning's meeting I suggested we should look at delivery systems. You said "great" and then promptly suggested a new advertising campaign and the rest of the meeting was spent discussing this. It would be very helpful if at the next meeting you could assist me in developing the idea of improved delivery systems. How do you feel about that?'

This time Susan has followed the constructive feedback guidelines. First, she acknowledges the positive influence that Steven has on the meeting. She provides very specific feedback on what Steven has done to cause the problem, proposes a solution, and seeks his agreement. A variation would be to ask Steven for *his* ideas on how to deal with the problem – especially since ideas are his forte!

Improving morale, motivation and commitment

Most writers on motivation emphasise that key factors are:

- recognition for a job well done
- a sense of achievement
- unlocking the potential for growth and development.

Constructive feedback is fundamental to achieving these aims. We have already discussed the importance of giving feedback for a job well done – as well as of saying when improvements are needed – and the key role that feedback plays in coaching, training, and developing potential. Being able to give and receive constructive feedback can also have a powerful effect on personal relationships. All these activities contribute to motivation and commitment.

Formal/informal feedback

Although we are keen to promote the idea that feedback is best received when it is given regularly and on an informal basis, there are two situations when the feedback must be formalised because of the potentially serious implications it may have. These two situations are:

- the formal (often annual) performance appraisal interview
- the conclusion of a formal disciplinary hearing.

Taking the formal performance review first, the outcomes from most appraisal schemes can have a direct impact on future salary and career progression, whether or not there are performance-related pay schemes in operation. We would suggest that managing performance is an activity that should happen every day. Formal systems, such as appraisal systems, just capture the outcomes of this ongoing constructive feedback process. Nothing should come as a surprise at the formal appraisal interview: the issues should have been raised and discussed around the time they occurred.

What happens when any counselling, coaching, or training proves ineffective and performance has become a more serious issue? This may be the stage when the formal disciplinary procedure is initiated. In many ways, the feedback process used in these situations is little different from that used in others. However, most disciplinary procedures are based on advice offered by the Advisory, Conciliation and Arbitration Service (ACAS)[2], which sets out the additional key principles that apply at every stage, ie that employees who are accused of failing to reach appropriate standards should:

- be entitled to know the complaint against them

- have their situation properly investigated

- have the opportunity of presenting their case

- know the standards they should be achieving and what support or training they can expect from their management

● know how long they have to reach the standard and how they will be reassessed

● know the implications of failing to reach the standard.

Common sense suggests that these principles are little more than a summary of what should have happened previously and are a clear indication of what will happen. It is important that the principles are applied fairly and reasonably, or they might be tested on appeal to senior management or an industrial tribunal.

In this chapter we have looked at the important role that constructive feedback plays in almost every aspect of working life. We also argue that constructive feedback is equally useful outside work – with one's family and one's friends. It is a true *lifeskill*.

We have also started to highlight some of the key themes that underlie constructive feedback, ie the need for:

● clear standards of performance

■ specific examples of behaviour or performance that need changing

▲ two-way communication to identify the issues and come up with solutions

● comments on positives as well as negatives.

We shall develop these themes in the next chapter.

Exercise 2

Reflect on the opportunities for you to give feedback, and record in your logbook:

- to whom you want to give feedback
- what feedback you want to give them.

References

1   BLANCHARD, KENNETH *and* SPENCER JOHNSON, *The One Minute Manager*. London, Fontana/Collins, 1983.

2   ADVISORY, CONCILIATION and ARBITRATION SERVICE. *Discipline at Work*. London, ACAS, 1989.

3 the 10 tools of giving constructive feedback

In the previous chapter we looked at situations where constructive feedback can make a real difference to people's performance and therefore, ultimately, to business success. In this chapter we concentrate on the skills of giving constructive feedback – offering the '10 Tools' for effective feedback.

1 Analyse the current situation

What is the problem? Be very clear what it is about the present behaviour or performance that needs changing, and why. Have examples ready: be able to describe what happened and what the consequences were. Prepare a case in a similar way to making a business proposal.

2 Decide on your outcome(s) and objective(s)

At the heart of any feedback session is the question of what both parties desire as the outcome of the feedback that passes between them. The first step is to clarify exactly what you want the feedback to achieve, and then to construct the strategy for the session around the desired outcome(s). Your objective should be:

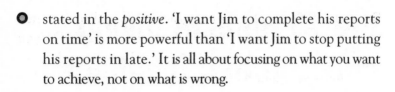 stated in the *positive*. 'I want Jim to complete his reports on time' is more powerful than 'I want Jim to stop putting his reports in late.' It is all about focusing on what you want to achieve, not on what is wrong.

■ *specific*. Fine-tune your objective; 'I want Jim to complete his quarterly review reports by the schedule of dates I have given him.'

▲ *achievable by you*. 'I want to encourage and help Jim to complete his quarterly review reports by the schedule of dates I have given him.' (Only Jim can actually complete the report; what you can do is help and support him.)

● accompanied by a clear statement of what some people call *measurable success evidence*, eg what you will see, hear, and feel when the report is completed on time. This is quite an easy example: it is straightforward to monitor whether a report is handed in on time. Some objectives are less tangible. For example, if the objective concerns Jim's ability to handle angry customers then it will be helpful to set out the behaviours that you expect Jim to display – such as maintaining good eye-contact and active listening.

● accompanied by a strong image or experience of *achieving the objective* – again, what will you see, hear, and feel when you achieve your objective. (This is very motivating: top sportspeople visualise or experience winning a particular event as a way of heightening performance.)

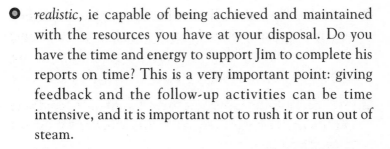

- *realistic*, ie capable of being achieved and maintained with the resources you have at your disposal. Do you have the time and energy to support Jim to complete his reports on time? This is a very important point: giving feedback and the follow-up activities can be time intensive, and it is important not to rush it or run out of steam.

- formed with an awareness of what might be *stopping* you from pursuing the objective and what the advantages might be of doing nothing. It could be that you feel your relationship with Jim might be damaged by giving the feedback. It is important to deal with this concern. What can you do to ensure that the relationship is not damaged?

- *worthwhile* in terms of the cost to you (eg in stress, money, and time) in striving for the objective. Is it a valuable use of your time?

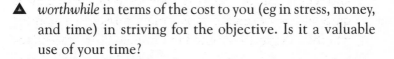

- set within a *timescale*.

Try it out for a feedback situation that is important for you. If you are clear about what you are trying to achieve with your feedback, so will the recipient be. However, remember that at this stage it is *your* objective. Be prepared to be flexible in the content or timing of the changes you are seeking. The aim is to have an objective to which you are both committed. Only the individual can change his or her behaviour or performance; at the end of the feedback session he or she must *own* the objective.

3 Calibrate for receptiveness

Just as different people have different tolerances for alcohol
or direct sunlight, so their capacity to accept feedback will
vary. This capacity may also change on a day-by-day basis,
depending on how they feel. Some writers describe this as
people behaving as 'buckets', 'tumblers', or 'thimbles'.

Buckets are ready and willing to receive feedback, and even
seek it out. They feel very confident in their ability to
improve and seem positively to welcome feedback. However,
Russell[1] warns against the 'bucket with a hole in', the person
who appears to want more feedback, but nothing changes;
the feedback goes in and comes out the hole in the bottom
'without touching the sides'. *Tumblers* are able to take a
reasonable amount of feedback – perhaps up to three or four
key pieces of information. *Thimbles* need careful attention.
Perhaps they feel insecure, doubt their ability to improve, or
have simply been damaged by receiving an undiluted diet of
criticism in the past. Thimbles will be able to take no more
than one piece of feedback at a time, so be gentle with them.

What is important is to recognise that people differ in their
capacity to absorb feedback (and an individual can be
different at different times). You need to calibrate them at
the outset and then, throughout your feedback session, by
paying close attention to their reactions, observing them and
listening actively to their responses, adjust the pace and
content of your feedback accordingly. You need to monitor

how full their bucket, tumbler, or thimble is. If the recipient is in any way limited in the amount he or she can take, prioritise and concentrate on the most important issues.

4 Create the right environment

Create the best environment for the feedback message to be understood and accepted. It is important to establish a supportive climate of trust, mutual respect, and openness for giving and receiving feedback. This is influenced by how well you know the person and what 'baggage' from previous encounters, good and bad, you both bring to the feedback session. The process is helped by:

- setting up a 'feedback contract' – the ground rules for your feedback relationship, which establish you as partners in the process. It is best to do this at the outset of a new relationship and before you have to give any feedback. You might say, 'It is important we are honest with each other. Please let me know if I am doing something that is not helpful to you or the team. Equally, I would like to be able to give you feedback. How do you feel about this?' This enables you to discuss the concept of giving feedback before you actually do so.

- the timing of the feedback session. Ideally, it should take place when both of you have sufficient time and are not under pressure. However, remember the golden rule: the session should come as soon as possible after the event that has led to the need for feedback.

▲ the place. It needs to be quiet and without interruptions.

● being in 'rapport' – getting to know and empathise with the recipient so that there is a sense of 'unconscious communication'. MacLennan[2] describes how Aristotle Onassis (a master rapport developer) would try to match every aspect of the person's behaviour – the way they spoke, their body language and breathing – by forcing himself to focus totally on the individual and coming to understand and appreciate them. You may feel that it is a bit extreme to try to match every part of a person's behaviour, and that he or she would see your trying to do so as a bit odd! However, you might give it a try by perhaps being upbeat if the other person is upbeat, or by toning it down a bit if he or she is a bit subdued. You may find that you automatically soften your voice when you deal with someone who speaks quietly, and vice versa. Some writers describe this as 'getting alongside people', or putting yourself in their shoes: being able to see, hear, and feel as they do and so being able to communicate better with them.

5 Communicate effectively

Use your communication skills. Remember:

● the three ways that a message is conveyed,

   O by what you say, ie the words you use (accounting for 7 per cent of the message)

☐ how you say it, ie the tone of your voice, the emphasis you put on different words, the volume of your voice, and the pace at which you speak (accounting for 38 per cent)

△ your body language, ie the expression on your face, the quality of eye-contact, and your body posture (accounting for 55 per cent).[3]

Many people find this a surprising result: the low importance of the words compared with the high importance of voice and body language. However, the effect of your feedback can be negated if the message conveyed through your words is not backed up by your voice and body language. For example, the statement 'Your presentation generally was good; however, you need to leave more time for questions' can come across as a supportive suggestion for change or, if delivered in an angry or sarcastic tone, as destructive criticism.

■ to listen actively and observe – to gather all the information and pick up all the signals from the recipient. Remember to:

○ give your full concentration (listening actively is hard)

☐ keep an open mind and avoid assumptions

△ keep calm – anger is a great barrier to listening

○ show you are listening by maintaining good eye-contact and nodding your head

○ reflect and summarise, using your own words to repeat what you have heard – again to show you are listening and to check you have understood the message correctly[4]

▲ to question effectively in order

○ to find information useful for understanding the issues, eg ask 'What is stopping you completing your reports on time? What specific information is proving difficult to obtain?'

□ to help the recipient work through the issues themselves. For example, ask 'What do you think is the impact on Jane of dropping her from the project team? How else could you have let Jane know her work for you was not up to standard?'

It is unusual to go into a feedback session with all the necessary information. If you think that you already have it, you are setting out to fail.[5]

6 Describe the behaviour you wish to change

This is a crucial stage. It is essential, first, that the person understands what the issue is; secondly, that he or she accepts there is a problem; and thirdly, that he or she accepts there is a need to change.

● Have examples that describe precisely what you saw or heard the person doing or saying, eg say 'You arrived late three times last week. On Monday, you said you were sick…'

■ Don't try to be a mind-reader, eg instead of saying 'You got very angry with that customer' say 'You were speaking very loudly and glaring at the customer.'

▲ Avoid such expressions as 'I don't like your attitude' or 'You are not committed enough.' What do you mean by 'attitude' or 'committed'? What exactly is the individual doing or saying? What is the behaviour that leads you to make that remark?

● Concentrate on behaviour and performance that can be changed. Avoid comments on personality like 'You need to be more bubbly, take things less seriously.'

● Explain what was the outcome of the behaviour, eg say 'The customer started to shout back and walked out without the complaint being resolved.'

● Try not to evaluate. Don't say 'It was a mistake to have raised that issue at the meeting when I was not there.' Instead, say 'Raising the issue at the meeting when I was not there meant that I was unable to explain the constraints on the timetable.' By leaving out your reaction or judgement you leave the individual more space to take on board the feedback.

■ Stay with the 'facts' or, when you do give your opinions, reactions, and perceptions present them as such, and be prepared to re-evaluate them in the light of the feedback that the individual gives you.

▲ Beware of putting the other person down or using

language that might cause defensiveness or an emotional reaction eg avoid saying 'How on earth could you have done something so stupid?'

7 Describe the behaviour you want

It is important to make clear what behaviour or performance you want from them in the future, eg say 'I want you to return customer calls within 24 hours.' Often performance is poor because people are not clear about the standards that are expected.

8 Seek solutions together

Making the required changes may not be easy and the individual may need help to make them. You may need to make some suggestions, eg if someone is always finishing projects late, suggest that they break the project down into individual tasks that can be scheduled. Whenever possible, try to encourage the individual to find solutions by asking 'What could you do differently?' and help him or her explore the problem areas by asking 'What is stopping you from doing the job?' You may need to help them evaluate the ideas: 'Will it achieve the desired result?…Is it within your control?…Are there any downsides?'

People may need your help – through coaching, your agreement for them to go on a training programme, or intervention with a third party. You must be prepared to give that help or explain why not. However, it is important that you do not help too much, eg by offering to write sections of the report that is always late.

9 Focus on what is good

Be sure to focus on the good as well as the not-so-good – the areas for improvement. Some people suggest the use of the 'good-bad-good sandwich', ie alternating the positive and negative messages so that:

- a 'good message' opens the learner to genuine communication, preventing him or her from switching off from what might be seen as criticism

- the 'bad message' is then delivered to effect the improvement in behaviour

- the final 'good message' sends the learner away feeling positive about the exchange.

10 Getting agreement

You cannot force someone to change his or her behaviour or performance. You can help and encourage, but only that person can make the change. Therefore, it is vital that the individual agrees:

- measurable, objective standards for the job or area of behaviour under discussion

■ there is a gap between current performance and what is required, the size of that gap, and the fact that he or she must 'own' the gap

▲ actions (eg behaviour change, training, and new procedures) to close the gap

● the timescales for achieving the change and, if it is a major change, review dates along the way.

Use the 10 Tools as a check-list to help you plan your feedback sessions. You can also use it to review your performance after a feedback session, ie to give yourself some feedback!

Exercise 3

Reflect on the 10 Tools and how you could apply them to specific feedback opportunities. Choose two or three of the opportunities you identified in Exercise 2 and record in your logbook:

○ your plan for the feedback sessions

▫ any further information you need.

References

1   RUSSELL, TIM. *Effective Feedback Skills*. London, Kogan Page, 1994.

2   MACLENNAN, NIGEL. *Coaching and Mentoring*. Aldershot, Gower, 1995.

3   MEHRABIAN, A. *and* FERRIS, I. 'Inference of attitudes from nonverbal communication in two channels,' *The Journal of Counselling Psychology*, Vol 31, 1967. pp 248–52.

4   MACKAY, IAN. *Listening Skills*. London, IPD, 1995.

5   MACKAY, IAN. *Asking Questions*. London, IPD, 1995.

challenging feedback situations

Whatever your situation, you will sometimes come up against people who are hard to get on with or difficult to 'manage'. Often a basic problem is that you find it difficult to give them feedback. We do not call this 'dealing with difficult people' but 'dealing with challenging feedback situations'. A play on words, perhaps? Yes, but it is important to see these situations not as ones to be dreaded but as opportunities to develop your feedback skills.

We would stress that, whatever the situation in which feedback is given, where feedback is an integral part of 'the way we do things round here' (ie the organisational culture) and is given continuously as small corrections to behaviour or performance, there is a lower chance that the recipient will go into shock and negative reaction.

Think about some feedback situations that you have found challenging and record the details in your logbook in the format used in the table on page 40.

We would guess that these situations are characterised not so much by the type of person you are dealing with, such as your boss or a fellow team member, but by the reactions you get to your feedback. Although every feedback situation will

I FIND THAT THE MOST CHALLENGING SITUATIONS ARE:			
NAME	RELATIONSHIP	WHAT WAS CHALLENGING ABOUT THE SITUATION?	WHAT WAS THE OUTCOME/ REACTION?

be different, there are certain 'reactions' that pose particular challenges. We shall look in detail at those where the person:

- ● disagrees with the feedback
- ■ is uninterested or not concerned
- ▲ is shocked, gets very upset, and perhaps cries
- ● becomes angry
- ● denies your right to give him or her feedback.

Understanding and preparing for challenging situations

The first step to understanding why such situations are so challenging is to consider why people behave in a way that makes it so difficult for you to give them constructive feedback. Possible reasons could be that they:

● lack confidence – they are afraid to confront their performance issues

■ feel under pressure and simply cannot take anything else on board

▲ are comfortable as they are – they do not want to be challenged

● see feedback as a challenge to their status or reputation

● see feedback as a power issue – if they accept feedback from you, it gives you power, whereas if they reject it or make it difficult for you to give feedback, it gives them power.

The list is endless. There are as many reasons as there are people and, in any case, people change, so that today's 'power freak' is tomorrow's 'change avoider'. However, understanding the reasons people behave in a particular way is invaluable in helping you deal with them.

We suggest that you plan and run your feedback sessions as set out in the 10 Tools (see Chapter 3). Here we are focusing on Tool 3: Calibrate for receptiveness. This is the part where you consider how much feedback an individual is likely to be able to take and, crucially, *how he or she might react*. It is difficult to deal with an unexpected reaction. The following sections will consider some of the more common reactions and suggest some strategies for dealing with them.

The person who disagrees with the feedback

Disagreement can occur in almost any feedback situation. It is important to be prepared for this reaction, because it is one of the most disconcerting. Your response will depend on whether the other person is disagreeing with the facts – the behaviours and performance you have described – or with the question of whether those behaviours are a problem. If he or she disagrees:

● with the facts, then

   O give as many examples as you can

   ☐ probe for the areas of disagreement, eg ask 'Are you disagreeing that the incident took place or only certain details of the incident?…Which details?'

   △ draw out his or her version of events, and then probe strongly around the differences, eg ask 'What specifically did you say to the customer the second time she returned the toaster?'

■ that a problem even exists, then explain why there is a problem by clarifying the consequences of their behaviour, eg if someone feels that the odd mistake on an invoice sent out does not matter ('Everyone makes mistakes') it will be helpful to explain what the customer reaction is and how that might affect the business.

▲ then keep an open mind. Is it possible that your 'facts' are inaccurate in some way? Be prepared perhaps to adjourn the feedback discussion and investigate further.

It will be impossible to move on until a measure of agreement is reached: acceptance that a problem does exist is the key first step along the path of change. It may sometimes be frustrating to have to 'waste' time dealing with these disagreements: *you* know there is a problem and want to get on and solve it. However, remember you cannot *make* people change their behaviour, they must *want* to do it. So be prepared to take time to deal with disagreement.

The person who is uninterested or not concerned

This situation is most likely to occur with a demotivated member of your staff, or perhaps with a colleague. These are the strategies you should use:

● Link your feedback strongly to performance standards and make clear that there is a gap in performance, eg say 'The company standard is that all letters should have a reply within three days; over the last month 50 per cent of your cases met this standard.'

■ Reinforce this message by indicating the impact of the substandard performance on departmental or organisational goals, eg say 'As a result the department is not meeting its target of an average time for reply of 2.5 days.'

▲ Although it is always helpful to involve the feedback recipient in finding solutions and setting targets or action plans, in this situation it is vital to engage the individual in the process and not allow him or her to be a passive party to the discussion.

◉ Get a clear commitment to the plan for change with firm timescales and, if appropriate, put it in writing.

◉ Follow up and, if necessary, follow up again and again!

The situation of total turnoff is likely to be too deeply rooted to be solved by a single 'chat'. However, you will note how the strategies suggested above can at least get a dialogue going. Persistence is going to be your greatest asset with Mr or Ms Totally-Uninterested.

The person who is shocked, gets very upset, and perhaps cries

If feedback is continuous and constructive it is unlikely that you will find yourself in the situation where the recipient gets very upset. However, with the best will in the world, this situation could well arise with a member of your staff or a colleague if you have not calibrated them accurately. For most of us it is the reaction we most dread: we find dealing with emotions in the workplace difficult. The strategies you need are these:

● For those in shock: show empathy. They have a right to be shocked. For example, say 'I understand that you are shocked if you have not heard this before.' Give them time to express their shock: they need to get it out of their system before you can move on to deal with the issue. Listening and empathising is important at this stage.

■ For those who cry:

○ give them 'permission' to do so. Many people feel embarrassed if they cry or show emotion and feel that it is not acceptable to 'break down' at work. For example, say 'It's OK to cry; take your time.'

□ give them time and space. Be prepared to talk about why they are finding the feedback so upsetting.

△ when they seem to have calmed down carry on gradually (all the time calibrating how they are feeling), judging the pace by their reactions.

○ try not to put off the session, even if it seems very tempting to do so. It is better to try to move forward into the positive part of the session – into finding solutions. Otherwise you may be leaving the individual with the problem and no support to deal with it.

The person who gets angry

This situation could arise with a colleague, or possibly when you are trying to give constructive feedback to a boss who feels it is not your place to give feedback. It may occur in situations when you have recently taken over as the manager, and particularly with members of your staff who have been in the job a long time. They have had years of being encouraged to believe that they have done a good job, and may look upon themselves as indispensable. They may be shocked and then angry if they receive feedback questioning the way they work. Anger can be very intimidating to deal with. So what do you do? The strategies are these:

● Empathise with their situation and acknowledge their right to be angry, while not agreeing that your feedback is misplaced, eg say 'I can understand why you are angry: what I have said must have come as a shock.'

■ Find something to agree with in what they say, eg 'I appreciate that you have been working very hard.'

▲ Do not be deflected (unless genuinely convinced): anger can be used very successfully as a weapon. How many people can you think of in your organisation whom everyone tries to avoid upsetting because their reaction can be so unpleasant?

Clearly it is even better to avoid setting off the angry reaction. If you are dealing with someone whom you know has a 'short fuse' or is super-sensitive to negative feedback, think about:

- setting up the feedback contract. You will recall that in Chapter 3 we suggested establishing at the outset of any relationship the fact that both partners are willing to give feedback to, and receive feedback from, each other. Ideally it is best to do this before you have to give any feedback. However, if you are not able to set up the contract in advance, it can still be a very useful way to start a feedback session when you are dealing with either a very sensitive issue or a very sensitive person.

- aligning your objectives with those of the person receiving the feedback. It is very useful if you can agree that you are working towards the same objective, eg to provide excellent customer care. This has the dual benefit of focusing on the positive side of what you are trying to achieve and also on providing an area of agreement at the outset.

It can take courage as well as skill to tackle the 'short fuse' individuals. However, it is a situation where feedback can have a powerful influence, because it is likely that these individuals have been working in a feedback 'desert'. Just as there can be a dramatic change when a desert has a shower of rain, with grass and flowers appearing almost overnight, the effect of feedback on these individuals can be equally dramatic. You may also find that they become your staunchest allies and most valued colleagues!

The person who denies your right to give him or her feedback

Denial can apply in a wide range of situations – perhaps most commonly with people who do not expect to be receiving feedback from you, such as your boss, colleagues in another department, or customers. Consider these relationships as two types: those where there is a close relationship with regular contact (eg your boss) and those where the relationship is more distant with less frequent contact (eg your customers). Taking the first type, the strategy is to:

● set up the feedback contract. Although the concepts of 'upwards' and '360-degree' feedback are much talked about at the moment, they are rarely implemented organisation-wide or on a systematic basis. Therefore, it is likely that the idea of giving feedback to your boss or colleague may be rather daunting. Setting up the feedback contract allows you to dip your toes gently into what might be dangerous waters.

The next two principles apply equally to both types of relationships:

● We pointed out in Chapter 2 that credibility in terms of your expertise to give feedback on a particular subject is vital. In situations where this may be in doubt (eg with your boss or a colleague in another department) or simply unknown (eg with your customers) it is essential to establish your credibility early on. Remind your boss that you have a lot of experience dealing with a particular subject. With customers, the best approach could be to remind them that you have very detailed knowledge of a particular procedure or product.

■ Again, aligning objectives can be a powerful technique – demonstrate the mutual advantage of addressing the issue. For example, when dealing with a customer who has complained about late deliveries, but who is actually causing the problem by putting in their orders late (and therefore you need to give them some feedback), it would be helpful to start by saying, 'I appreciate that it is very important for you to receive the deliveries to fit in with your production schedules. Our objective is to provide the best possible service to you and I am really keen to work with you to meet your delivery needs.' This puts the spotlight on what you want to achieve and away from the issue of unsolicited or unwanted feedback. It opens the way for your constructive feedback.

We have set out some useful techniques and principles for dealing with the types of feedback situation that you may find most challenging. Thinking through the strategies that you could adopt will make you not only better prepared to deal with these situations, but will also give you the confidence to tackle them. Used in conjunction with the 10 Tools, it should ensure some very constructive feedback sessions.

Exercise 4

Reflect on the strategies for dealing with challenging feedback situations. For the feedback opportunities developed in Exercise 3 complete your planning and record in your logbook:

○ how you think the recipients will react

▫ what strategies you plan to use.

Go for it!

receiving feedback

So far we have considered *your* giving feedback to someone else, and how you might develop your skills in giving feedback constructively. It is equally important to develop your skills in *receiving* feedback, because:

● to perform effectively, and to grow and develop, you too need feedback

■ if you give feedback you must be prepared to receive feedback. This is part of the feedback contract, whether set up formally or not.

Do we receive feedback?

It is worth considering at this stage:

● how much feedback you receive now

■ who gives you feedback and who does not

▲ how constructive the feedback is that you receive

● how you feel about receiving feedback.

We talked earlier about the feedback desert. Not many plants can survive, let alone flourish, in desert conditions, and the same is true of people. Yet it is surprising how many people might answer 'not a lot' to the first point posed above. Surely, though, at least your boss will give you feedback? Possibly he or she will at the annual appraisal, but what about on a regular basis? How many bosses, if you asked them to give you more feedback, might say: 'If you have to ask how you are getting on, you can't be doing very well!' or 'Don't worry, I will tell you when you are going wrong.'

Both of these situations actually happened to one of the authors, and left him feeling concerned. Had he actually got it right – was he really doing well? Or was his performance just OK and, unless he improved it in some (as yet unspecified) way, was it likely to slip to a level where remedial action would be required? How could he improve his performance to go beyond being OK?

What about other colleague team members or the staff working for you? Are you perhaps aware that a relationship is not quite right but you do not know why? It can come as a shock to find there is a problem and that it has been brewing for some time. The feedback that then results is often far from constructive, because it happens when someone has got so frustrated that his or her fear or dislike of giving feedback is overtaken by the need to do something. In the workplace you will often have to contend with receiving poor-quality feedback and what we have described as destructive criticism. We shall give you some tips later in this chapter for dealing with these situations.

The last question we posed above was how you feel about receiving feedback. You may reply 'Well, it all depends whether it is given constructively, who it is from', etc. However, it is important to think about this issue and calibrate yourself to discover how receptive you are to feedback. Is there anything stopping you seeking feedback or causing you to send out signals that you are not too keen to receive it? For example, do you:

● feel you have 'failed' and get very upset when anyone suggests your performance is not up to standard?

▩ avoid giving anyone the opportunity to criticise you in case it has an adverse affect on your career?

▲ worry that you may not be able to improve your performance?

◉ feel that there is no need for feedback – that everything is fine?

◉ feel embarrassed when someone is commenting either positively or negatively about you?

● feel hesitant about seeking feedback?

Accepting that you have barriers to receiving feedback is the first step. Then you need to think through how real those barriers are and start to reframe them into a more positive form. Focus on the advantages of receiving feedback: the opportunity to learn and grow, to deal with issues before they become a problem, and to improve and develop relationships.

Some people refer to feedback as a 'gift'; we feel that this is a really useful metaphor. We associate gifts with receiving something of value that gives us pleasure. What a different perspective it gives feedback if we see it as a gift! There is also evidence that seeking feedback actually creates a positive impression. Are you a bucket yet?

From whom do you need or want feedback?

So, from whom do we need feedback? Well, anyone and everyone really – in fact the more the better. However, we need it most from those whose opinion we value most and those who can have the greatest influence on our development. For example, if you are an aspiring young musician there is a greater chance you will be influenced by someone who has achieved a degree of fame as a musician than from someone who has never played a note. Similarly, if you are a sales assistant you are more likely to value feedback on your customer care skills from someone whose customer care skills you admire. Usually our bosses, spouses, and partners rate highly on our 'need-for-feedback' scale.

However, you may be less willing to accept feedback from your staff, feeling that it threatens your position as manager. Yet it is likely that it is with your staff that you have the most contact. They are ideally placed to comment on your performance, particularly as a 'people manager'. Can you afford to do without such a valuable source of information? Similarly, close colleagues or other team members can provide

Chartered Institute of Personnel and Development

Customer Satisfaction Survey

We would be grateful if you could spend a few minutes answering these questions and return the postcard to CIPD. <u>*Please use a black pen to answer.*</u> **If you would like to receive a free CIPD pen, please include your name and address.** IPD MEMBER Y/N

....

1. Title of book ....

2. Date of purchase: month ....   year ....

3. How did you acquire this book?
☐ Bookshop   ☐ Mail order   ☐ Exhibition   ☐ Gift   ☐ Bought from Author

4. If ordered by mail, how long did it take to arrive:
☐ 1 week   ☐ 2 weeks   ☐ more than 2 weeks

5. Name of shop ....   Town...   Country ....

6. Please grade the following according to their influence on your purchasing decision with 1 as least influential: (please tick)

	1	2	3	4	5
Title					
Publisher					
Author					
Price					
Subject					
Cover					

7. On a scale of 1 to 5 (with 1 as poor & 5 as excellent) please give your impressions of the book in terms of: (please tick)

	1	2	3	4	5
Cover design					
Paper/print quality					
Good value for money					
General level of service					

8. Did you find the book:

Covers the subject in sufficient depth   ☐ Yes   ☐ No
Useful for your work   ☐ Yes   ☐ No

9. Are you using this book to help:
☐ In your work ☐ Personal study   ☐ Both   ☐ Other (please state)

Please complete if you are using this as part of a course

10. Name of academic institution...

11. Name of course you are following? ....

12. Did you find this book relevant to the syllabus? ☐ Yes ☐ No ☐ Don't know

Thank you!

To receive regular information about CIPD books and resources call 020 8263 3387.

Any data or information provided to the CIPD for the purposes of membership and other Institute activities will be processed by means of a computer database or otherwise. You may, from time to time, receive business information relevant to your work from the Institute and its other activities. If you do not wish to receive such information please write to the CIPD, giving your full name, address and postcode. The Institute does not make its membership lists available to any outside organisation.

1795/05/00

Publishing Department
Chartered Institute of Personnel and Development
CIPD House
Camp Road
Wimbledon
London
SW19 4BR

a unique perspective on your skills, perhaps as a teamworker or in terms of your communication abilities. Do not forget your customers and suppliers: they too can be a powerful source of feedback on performance. The message is that feedback is valuable from everyone.

How to get constructive feedback

If the problem is that you are not getting feedback at all, or at least from certain key people, then ask for it! If this sounds embarrassing and you are tempted to forget the whole idea, then first consider what you are going to gain: lots of valuable information to help you improve your performance. Remember also that you have a right to feedback – everyone does. So, as with *giving* feedback, make a plan:

- Decide on the outcome(s) you want: what it is you want feedback on and why?

- Calibrate your 'feeder-back'. Do they have time to give you feedback now? How motivated or interested are they in giving you feedback on this particular subject?

- Forewarn your 'feeder-back' that you are looking for their help. This gives them time to think about the feedback they will give you and also the opportunity to express any concerns about giving the feedback, such as feeling that they are not the right person or that they do not have the time at present.

● Calibrate your receptiveness to feedback (are you a bucket, tumbler, or thimble?). If you are a thimble, this may not be the best time for you.

● Use your communication skills: get into rapport, listen actively, and be prepared to question effectively.

● Be specific about the help you need, eg say 'Will you help me get the right structure for my report?' rather than ask them to judge you by saying 'What do you think of my report?'

■ Beware of asking leading questions, eg 'You thought my last presentation went all right, didn't you?'

▲ Act on the things you agree with, be prepared to discuss the things you do not agree with or do not understand, and keep an open mind – it is just possible they have a point.

Try it. Make a list of issues on which you feel you would benefit from receiving feedback, and of the people who could help you. Notice the effect on them when you make it clear that you are interested in and value their feedback and notice the effect that opening up this communication has on your relationships with those people. We believe that unblocking the feedback channels can have benefits that go well beyond the immediate subject area of the feedback. It can improve and strengthen communication, relationships, and morale generally.

How to deal with the less constructive feedback

You might give *us* feedback on this book so far by saying something like, 'Well, it's all right for you to talk about getting people to give you constructive feedback, but you have never met my boss/team/husband/wife. My problem is that everybody and anybody sees it as fair game to tell me everything that is wrong with me. Positive feedback I can take, but what about all the rest?' So how might you deal with the rest of the world who have not read this book? Here are a few tips on converting that *criticism* into constructive feedback:

● Identify what *their* motives are in giving you this particular feedback at this particular time.

■ Take control of your thoughts (you are probably feeling rather depressed or angry with the feedback you are receiving) by seeking the positive intent behind apparently negative words. It may well be that they are trying to help you improve your performance despite sounding like they are attacking you. Whether this is the case or not, perceiving the feedback in this more positive way will help you deal with it.

▲ If the feedback is subjective or directed at your personality or attitude, use your questioning skills to move the feedback on to the real issues by seeking examples: 'You are saying that I don't get on with the rest of the team. Can you give me some examples of what I am doing that is causing a problem?' Then keep the discussion focused on the issues.

- Similarly, if the feedback is rather vague, probe for more details, eg say 'I understand you are telling me my report is not meeting the marketing manager's needs. Can you be more specific about what the marketing manager wants that is not being met by my report?' Go on probing until you are crystal-clear about the issues.

- If the 'feeder-back' is angry or aggressive, first empathise with him or her, eg by saying, 'I understand you are angry that I did not consult you about... .' Your next move depends on whether you feel that the feedback is justified. If you feel it is not, you may wish to explain why you did not consult. In either circumstance, quickly move the discussion on to the future, eg by saying, 'How can we ensure this does not happen again?' or 'How would you like me to handle this next time?' In the face of continuing anger, keep focusing on the detail of what can be done differently. Having a strategy and concentrating on the issues rather than the angry response will help you to keep calm and take control of the discussion.

- Help yourself with the *way* the feedback is delivered by summarising the other person's criticism and reflecting it back in your own *constructive* words.

- Remind yourself that if someone is taking the trouble to give you feedback then the change could be worthwhile.

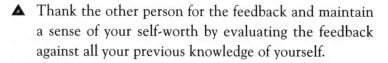 Thank the other person for the feedback and maintain a sense of your self-worth by evaluating the feedback against all your previous knowledge of yourself.

● Decide next what outcome(s) you want from hearing this feedback. If a change in your performance is required, decide what to do differently in order to achieve your outcome – plan it out.

● Visualise the successful outcome of that change; it will help motivate you to make the changes.

● Go out and implement your plan, making sure to review your progress.

■ Give feedback on the outcome to your 'feeder-back'!

Above all, keep reminding yourself that feedback is a gift. You do not have to accept the feedback without question, but you owe it to yourself to think about it and evaluate it. Only you can make the decision to change your performance. If you decide to reject the feedback, it is important to let the 'feeder-back' know both this and the reasons for your decision – to complete the feedback loop. Otherwise, far from improving, relationships are likely to deteriorate.

The ability to receive and handle feedback is just as vital a skill as that of giving feedback. They are two sides of the same coin. They both need practice and you will learn from every feedback experience. The next chapter will help you make the most of this learning and help you continuously improve your feedback skills.

Exercise 5

Reflect on the opportunities to receive feedback, and record in your logbook:

o the areas of performance on which you would like to receive feedback

▫ who is best placed to give you that feedback

△ your plan.

Go out and get it!

---

continuously improving your feedback skills

Developing your skills in giving and receiving constructive feedback is almost like adopting a new lifestyle. As you become sensitised to the concept of feedback, you will suddenly become aware that you are giving and receiving feedback in some form almost all the time. In addition to the more 'formal' feedback sessions that you plan for, there will be numerous occasions when you find yourself either giving or receiving feedback informally, be it just mentioning to a member of your staff that it would be useful in future to include x on the circulation list for the team-meeting minutes, or commenting to your nearest and dearest that you would like him or her to put the top on the shampoo bottle! These everyday encounters dealing with perhaps quite minor issues (or at least minor from your perspective) are all opportunities to practise your feedback skills. You may be surprised at the benefits – minor issues have a habit of turning into 'World War III' for no apparent good reason. However, the 'good reason' is that your member of staff actually sees your comment as a criticism of his or her performance on circulating the minutes; your nearest and dearest thinks you are fussing over nothing, feels annoyed, and as a result does nothing.

Developing any skill needs two key ingredients: the opportunity to practise and feedback on progress. In the case of developing your feedback skills, it may be possible to get 'feedback on our feedback' from others (and this is always worth seeking!), but very often you will have to rely on your own perceptions. The best way to do this is to review what has happened and set up a system to give yourself some constructive feedback on the continuous improvement of your feedback skills. You might find it helpful to use a structured format, as set out below in our Reflections Sheets, comparing the outcome(s) with the objective(s), identifying what has worked well, and why; what has not worked so well, and why not. Finally, and most importantly, be clear about what you have learned from the experience and what you will do differently next time.

The 10 Tools in Chapter 3 and the strategies for dealing with challenging situations are there for guidance, not as rules to be followed blindly. By trying out different approaches for different people you can identify which of our Tools are, for you, written in stone, and which are guidance to be used with discretion.

Reflection sheet: giving feedback

What were my objective(s)?

What was the outcome?

What went well and why?

What went less well and why?

What have I learned?

What will I do differently next time?

Reflection sheet: receiving feedback

Did I seek it?   **Yes/No**   **If No, how might I have sought it?**

If Yes, what were my objectives?   **If No, what were the 'feeder-back's' objectives?**

What was the outcome?

What went well and why?

What went less well and why?

What have I learned?

What will I do differently next time?

Exercise 6

Reflect on your experiences of giving and receiving feedback and record in your logbook:

- ⊙ your completed reflection sheets

- ▣ what further help you need in developing your feedback skills.

Good luck!

There are three messages that come across consistently in our research. The first is the great personal sense of learning that comes from *giving* constructive feedback. This seems strange when you consider you usually set out to give feedback in order to develop the other person. The second point is the great sense of job satisfaction that comes when the feedback you have offered, whether formally as a manager or informally as a friend and colleague, has been taken on board and has led to improved performance. Thirdly, what a powerful force giving and receiving feedback constructively can have on relationships, and on morale and motivation.

Good luck with developing your skills. Oh, by the way, do not forget to give us constructive feedback via the Institute of Personnel and Development on your response to this book. We guarantee to take it into account in any revisions we make.

appendices

Useful videos

There are a few videos focusing specifically on feedback skills and some addressed at performance management/appraisals, coaching and counselling. A selection is set out below.

Constructive Criticism, from Fenman.

Feedback Solutions, from Melrose.

Feedback Techniques, from Fenman.

I'd Like a Word With You, from Video Arts.

Further reading

BRAMSON R. M. *Dealing with Difficult Bosses*. London, Nicholas Brealey Publishing, 1992.

BRAMSON R. M. *Dealing with Difficult People*. New York, Ballentine Books, 1981.

CLUTTERBUCK D. *Everyone Needs a Mentor: Fostering talent at work*. 2nd edn. London, IPD, 1991.

FELDER L. *Does Someone at Work Treat You Badly?: How to handle brutal bosses, crazy co-workers and anyone else who drives you nuts*. New York, Berkeley Books, 1993.

FISHER R. *and* URY W. *Getting to Yes: Negotiating agreement without giving in.* New York, Penguin Books, 1991.

O'CONNOR, J. *and* SEYMOUR, J. *Introducing NLP.* London, Aquarian Press, 1993. (See pp19–23 for rapport building.)

PARSLOE E. *The Manager as Coach and Mentor.* London, IPD, 1995.

Other titles in the *Management Shapers* series:

The Appraisal Discussion

Terry Gillen

The Appraisal Discussion shows you how to make appraisal a productive and motivating experience for all levels of performer – and help your credibility in the process! Practical advice is given on:

- assessing performance fairly and accurately

- using feedback, including constructive criticism and targeted praise, to improve performance

- ▲ handling 'difficult' appraisees

- encouraging and supporting reluctant appraisees

- setting, and gaining commitment to, worthwhile objectives

- avoiding common appraiser problems from inadvertent bias to 'appraisal speak'

- identifying ways to develop appraisees so they add value to the organisation.

First Edition
96 pages
Pbk
0 85292 751 7
1998
£5.95

Asking Questions

Ian MacKay

Asking Questions will help you ask the 'right' questions, using the correct form to elicit a useful response. All managers need to hone their questioning skills, whether interviewing, appraising or simply exchanging ideas. This book offers guidance and helpful advice on:

- using various forms of open questions – including probing, simple interrogative, opinion-seeking, hypothetical, extension and precision etc.

- encouraging and drawing out speakers through supportive statements and interjections

- establishing specific facts through closed or 'direct' approaches

- avoiding counter-productive questions

- using questions in a training context.

Second Edition
96 pages
Pbk
0 85292 768 1
November 1998
£5.95

Assertiveness

Terry Gillen

Assertiveness will help you feel naturally confident, enjoy the respect of others and easily establish productive working relationships, even with 'awkward' people. It covers:

- understanding why you behave as you do and, when that behaviour is counter-productive, knowing what to do about it

- understanding other people better

- keeping your emotions under control

- preventing others bullying, flattering or manipulating you against your will

- acquiring easy-to-learn techniques that you can use immediately

- developing your personal assertiveness strategy.

First Edition
96 pages
Pbk
0 85292 769 X
November 1998
£5.95

The Disciplinary Interview

Alan Fowler

The Disciplinary Interview will ensure you adopt the correct procedures, conduct productive interviews and manage the outcome with confidence. It offers step-by-step guidance on the whole process, including:

- understanding the legal implications

- investigating the facts

- presenting the management case

- probing the employee's case

- diffusing conflict through skilful listening and questioning

- distinguishing between conduct and competence

- weighing up the alternatives – dismissing or dropping the case; disciplining and improving performance through counselling and training.

First Edition
96 pages
Pbk
0 85292 753 3
1998
£5.95

Leadership Skills

John Adair

Leadership Skills will give you confidence, guide and inspire you on your journey from being an effective manager to becoming a leader of excellence. Acknowledged as a world authority on leadership, Adair offers stimulating insights on:

- recognising and developing your leadership qualities

- acquiring the personal authority to give positive direction and the flexibility to embrace change

- acting on the key interacting needs – to achieve your task, build your team and develop its members

- transforming the core leadership functions such as planning, communicating and motivating, into practical skills you can master.

First Edition
96 pages
Pbk
0 85292 764 9
November 1998
£5.95

Listening Skills

Ian MacKay

Listening Skills describes techniques and activities to improve your ability and makes clear why effective listening is such a crucial management skill – and yet so often overlooked or neglected. Clear explanations will help you:

- recognise the inhibitors to listening

- improve your physical attention so you are seen to be listening

- ▲ listen to what is really being said by analysing and evaluating the message

- ask the right questions so you understand what is not being said

- interpret tone of voice and non-verbal signals.

Second Edition
96 pages
Pbk
0 85292 754 1
1998
£5.95

Making Meetings Work

Patrick Forsyth

Making Meeting Work will maximise your time – both before and during meetings – clarify your aims, improve your own and others' performance and make the whole process rewarding and productive – never frustrating and futile. The book is full of practical tips and advice on:

- drawing up objectives and setting realistic agendas

- deciding the who, where and when to meet

- chairing effectively – encouraging discussion, creativity and sound decision-making

- sharpening your skills of observation, listening and questioning to get across your points

- dealing with problem participants

- handling the follow-up – turning decisions into action.

First Edition
96 pages
Pbk
0 85292 765 7
November 1998
£5.95

Motivating People

Iain Maitland

Motivating People will help you maximise individual and team skills to achieve personal, departmental and, above all, organisational goals. It provides practical insights on:

- becoming a better leader and co-ordinating winning teams
- identifying, setting and communicating achievable targets
- empowering others through simple job improvement techniques
- encouraging self-development, defining training needs and providing helpful assessment
- ensuring pay and workplace conditions make a positive contribution to satisfaction and commitment.

First Edition
96 pages
Pbk
0 85292 766 5
November 1998
£5.95

Negotiating, Persuading and Influencing

Alan Fowler

Negotiating, Persuading and Influencing will help you develop
the critical skills you need to manage your staff effectively,
bargain successfully with colleagues or deal tactfully with
superiors – thus ensuring that a constructive negotiation
process leads to a favourable outcome. Sound advice and
practical guidance is given on:

- recognising and using sources of influence

- probing and questioning techniques to discover the other
  person's viewpoint

- adopting collaborative or problem-solving approaches

- timing your tactics and using adjournments

- conceding and compromising to find common ground

- resisting manipulative ploys

- securing and implementing agreement.

First Edition
96 pages
Pbk
0 85292 755 X
1998
£5.95

The Selection Interview

Penny Hackett

The Selection Interview will ensure you choose better people – more efficiently. It provides step-by-step guidance on techniques and procedures from the initial decision to recruit through to the critical final choice. Helpful advice is included on:

- drawing up job descriptions, employee specifications and assessment plans

- setting up the interview

- using different interview strategies and styles

- improving your questioning and listening skills

- evaluating the evidence to reach the best decision.

First Edition
96 pages
Pbk
0 85292 756 8
1998
£5.95

Working in Teams

Alison Hardingham

Working in Teams looks at teamworking from the inside. It will give you invaluable insights into how you can make a more positive and effective contribution – as team member or team leader – to ensure your team works together and achieves together. Clear and practical guidelines are given on:

- understanding the nature and make-up of teams

- finding out if your team is on track

- overcoming the most common teamworking problems

- recognising your own strengths and weaknesses as a team member

- giving teams the tools, techniques and organisational support they need.

First Edition
96 pages
Pbk
0 85292 767 3
November 1998
£5.95